CULTURE IN ACTION

Will Smith

Liz Miles

Chicago, Illinois

www.heinemannraintree.com
Visit our website to find out more information about Heinemann-Raintree books.

To order:
☎ Phone 888-454-2279
💻 Visit www.heinemannraintree.com to browse our catalog and order online.

Edited by Louise Galpine and Rachel Howells
Designed by Kimberly Miracle and Betsy Wernert
Original illustrations © Capstone Global Library Ltd.
Illustrated by kja-artists.com
Picture research by Mica Brancic and Kay Altwegg
Production by Alison Parsons
Originated by Steve Walker, Capstone Global Library Ltd
Printed in China by Leo Paper Products Ltd

13 12 11 10 09
10 9 8 7 6 5 4 3 2 1

Library of Congress Cataloging-in-Publication Data
Miles, Liz.
  Will Smith / Liz Miles.
    p. cm. -- (Culture in action)
  Includes bibliographical references and index.
  ISBN 978-1-4109-3397-3 (hc) -- ISBN 978-1-4109-3414-7 (pb) 1. Smith, Will, 1968---Juvenile literature. 2. Actors--United States--Biography--Juvenile literature. 3. Rap musicians--United States--Biography--Juvenile literature. I. Title.
  PN2287.S612M55 2009
  791.4302'8092--dc22
  [B]
                    2008054320

Acknowledgments

The author and publishers are grateful to the following for permission to reproduce copyright material: p. 24 (Album/Zade Rosenthal/Columbia Pictures Corp./Escape Artists/Overbrook Entertainment); Corbis p. 28 (© Neal Preston); Getty Images pp. 4 (AFP/Timothy A. Clary), 8 (S. Granitz/WireImage), 9 (Don Murray), 10 (Michael Ochs Archives), 12 (David Drapkin/ImageDirect), 13 (Michael Ochs Archive/Lisa Haun), 14 (Hulton Archive/Darlene Hammond), 17 (Stone/Ken Biggs), 26 (Soul Brother/FilmMagic), 27 (Steve Granitz/WireImage); Macarthur O. Littles and the Class of 1968 p. 7 (http://www.overbrookhighreunion.com); Photolibrary p. 6; Redferns p. 11 (Echoes Archives); Rex Features p. 22 (Everett/20th Century Fox); The Kobal Collection pp. 5 (Relativity Media/Overbrook Entertainment), 16 (NBC/Stuffed Dog/Quincy Jones Ent), 18 (Warner Bros), 20 (MGM/Maiden/New Regency/Myles Aronowitz), 21 (Columbia/Frank Connor), 23 (Columbia/Melinda Sue Gordon), 29 (Dreamworks).

Icon and banner images supplied by Shutterstock: © Alexander Lukin, © ornitopter, © Colorlife, and © David S. Rose.

Cover photograph of a still from the film *I, Robot* reproduced with permission of The Kobal Collection (20th Century Fox).

We would like to thank Jackie Murphy and Nancy Harris for their invaluable help in the preparation of this book.

Every effort has been made to contact copyright holders of material reproduced in this book. Any omissions will be rectified in subsequent printings if notice is given to the publishers.

All the Internet addresses (URLs) given in this book were valid at the time of going to press. However, due to the dynamic nature of the Internet, some addresses may have changed, or sites may have changed or ceased to exist since publication. While the author and publishers regret any inconvenience this may cause readers, no responsibility for any such changes can be accepted by either the author or the publishers.

Contents

Some words are printed in bold, **like this**. You can find out what they mean by looking in the glossary on page 30.

Many Successes

Will Smith's life has been a list of successes. He always puts a ton of energy into anything he does. He once said, "When I was young I realized that the person that works the hardest wins." He is known as a perfectionist, which means he wants to do everything in a perfect way. He aims to do the best he can and tries to win people's admiration.

Many talents

Will Smith is unusual because he has been able to move easily from one art form to another—and then to another. He has been a successful pop singer, television actor, movie actor, and **producer**. Few people are skilled actors and singers, and even fewer are successful at both.

Will Smith ran two careers side by side. While a movie star, he was a singer, too.

Will's latest success is being a movie producer. Here he is on the set of *Hancock*, a movie he produced in 2007–08.

Sometimes, he has done more than one job at the same time. In 1997, for example, he had a leading role in the movie *Men in Black*. He also sang the main song for the movie.

Charming

This extraordinary performer makes people feel at ease. His friendliness, humor, and charm have helped him make some famous friends, such as Tom Cruise. People like to work with him because they know he always does his best. His supportive fans are people of all ages and races.

Leading the way

Will Smith is one of few African-Americans to get a lead role in a series of blockbuster movies. He is an **inspiration** to many African-American actors because white actors are more likely to be offered the star parts in movies.

Early Influences

Will's full name is Willard Christopher Smith Jr. He was born on September 25, 1968, in the city of Philadelphia, Pennsylvania. There was nothing special about the neighborhood where he was born. The area was called Winfield. The people who lived there were neither rich nor poor.

Will's family

Will's father, Willard Smith Sr., owned a company that sold freezers to supermarkets. Will's mother, Caroline, worked for the local school. Will was the second eldest of four children. He had an older sister, Pamela, and a younger brother and sister who were twins. Their names were Ellen and Harry.

Will was born in the suburbs of the city of Philadelphia.

"The Prince"

At school, Will was often the center of attention. He was always asking questions and cracking jokes. His charm often got him out of trouble. Teachers forgave him if he forgot his homework or was late because he was so polite and funny.

Will's friends and teachers began to call him "Prince Charming." This was shortened to "The Prince." Will later added "Fresh" to his nickname—he called himself the "Fresh Prince."

Worries

Will was not always sure of himself. He worried that his ears stuck out too much. "One guy once told me that I looked like a car with the doors open," he said. He used his jokes to stop bullies from picking on him.

This is Overbrook High School, where Will went to school.

A strict father

Will's parents were pretty strict. His father used to be in the Air Force. He taught Will the self-discipline (how to control behavior and work hard) he had learned. As a boy, Will did not like that his father was so strict, but self-discipline became a useful tool on his road to success. Will said, "I was so petrified of my parents that I managed to avoid most of the pitfalls that teens fall in."

Will Smith is pictured with his father, Will Smith Sr. Will's father taught him many useful lessons.

You can do anything

Will's father taught him that he could do anything if he really wanted to. One day, Will Sr. told Will and his brother to rebuild the brick wall in front of his business. Will and his brother did not think they could mix so much cement and lay so many bricks. After they had finished, Will's father said, "Don't you ever tell me there's something you can't do."

Will often saw his father installing freezers in supermarket basements, among rats and mud. It was a lesson for Will. Will wanted to make sure he never had to work near rats and mud.

Teenage temptations

Crime and drugs were common in parts of Philadelphia. Will's father worried that these things might tempt his teenage son. To keep him away from it, Will Sr. drove Will around the poorer parts of Philadelphia. Seeing homeless people and drug addicts warned Will to stay away from crime and drugs.

Will's father drove Will around the poorer parts of the city to see the misery caused by drugs and poverty.

Fresh Prince

When Will was still at school, a new style of music was becoming more and more popular. It was called **hip-hop** music. A few years later, hip-hop would be a major part of Will's life.

Rap

Hip-hop music began with **rap** in the 1970s in New York City. Rap is sort of like poetry, except it always **rhymes** and always has a strong, fast **rhythm**. The words are often about the rapper's life. They also give the rapper's opinions on different topics. While rapping, a drumbeat is often played in the background.

The Sugarhill Gang made the first successful rap/hip-hop record.

In the 1970s **DJs** would play beats from a song, such as a rock song. While playing the recorded beat, they or others rapped. At first, rap became popular with young people who were fed up with **disco music**. It was especially popular among African-Americans who lived in New York City.

The first rap **single** was "Rapper's Delight" (1979) by The Sugarhill Gang. Will heard this song on the radio when he was 11 years old. As soon as he heard it, he started rapping, too.

A musician in Grandmaster Flash and the Furious Five was the first person to use the term "hip-hop."

Hip-hop music

By the 1980s rap had reached other countries. Rap became known as hip-hop music. Today, hip-hop is a culture (way of life) for many young people. It has its own music, fashion, and art.

Starting in the early 1980s, when he was 13, Will spent his spare time as a rap DJ at parties. He rapped between records. He was influenced by the style of a hip-hop band named Grandmaster Flash and the Furious Five.

DJ Jazzy Jeff

In 1984, when he was 16, Will went to a party where Jazzy Jeff, a well-known DJ, was playing. Will asked if he could rap with him. DJ Jazzy Jeff agreed, and they quickly became friends. They started to perform together at parties and called themselves DJ Jazzy Jeff and the Fresh Prince.

Rock the House

The duo sent tapes of their music to a record **producer** in Philadelphia. He gave them to a local record company. The company made their first single, "Girls Ain't Nothing But Trouble." The record was played in a lot of clubs in Philadelphia.

A year before Will graduated from high school, a much bigger company called Jive Records heard the duo's record. They paid Will and Jeff $15,000 each for the rights to sell it. Very soon, it was a hit, and 100,000 copies were sold.

In 1987, just two weeks before Will finished high school, the duo's first **album** was released. It was called *Rock the House,* and 600,000 copies sold quickly. Will and Jeff went on tour and were amazed to be met by crowds of fans. They were famous!

Not serious enough?

The duo's music was about young people's worries and the fun they had. Often, it was funny. Other rappers did not always like their music. They didn't think it was serious enough. They preferred rap music that was about gangs and street-life. They thought rap music should talk angrily about the problems faced by African-Americans.

Hip-hop bands such as Public Enemy have hard-hitting, political lyrics. Will and Jeff's lyrics were more fun.

Even though some rap fans did not like their music, Will and Jeff had huge success. In 1989 they won the first-ever **Grammy** for a rap record. The song was called "Parents Just Don't Understand."

Here today, gone tomorrow

By the time Will was 18, he had $2 million and eight cars. By the time he was 21, he had nothing left! He had spent too much money on having a good time. Also, he had a big **tax** bill to pay.

In 1990, with a debt to pay and falling record sales, Will decided to try a new career. He wanted to be an actor, so he moved to Los Angeles.

Summertime

In 1991 Will worked with Jeff on their final album, *Homebase*. The single "Summertime" won them a second Grammy. DJ Jazzy Jeff and the Fresh Prince made music together until 1993. In 1997 Will recorded an album of his own called *Big Willie Style*.

Will is pictured at a music award ceremony with singer Celine Dion.

Rap rhythms

Listen to a variety of rap beats and try to clap them out at the same time. A rhythm is made up of strong beats and weak beats. Here is an example (the strong beats are in *italic*):

Jack and *Jill* went *up* the *hill*.

Now try writing your own rap lyrics.

Steps to follow:

1. Pick a subject you like a lot, such as buying a pair of new shoes or taking a vacation.

2. The lines in a rap usually rhyme (for example, "shoes" rhymes with "news"). Jot down some words about your subject that rhyme.

3. Write a good first line that has a strong beat. Clap out the beat.

4. Write a second line with a similar beat. Try to make the last word of the first and second lines rhyme.

5. Keep going until you've finished four to six lines. Each pair of lines could have a different rhyme.

Clap out the beat to some of Will Smith's music, such as Will and Jeff's "Parents Just Don't Understand."

Here's an example:

I *went* to the *mall* and I've *got* some *news*
I *bought* a *pair* of *cool* new *shoes*.

The Fresh Prince of Bel-Air

Will moved to Los Angeles, the movie-making center of the United States. He hoped that his fame would help him get an acting job.

A lucky meeting

Will had a lucky meeting with a record **producer** named Benny Medina. Benny had an idea for a television comedy series. He thought that Will would be good in it. Benny persuaded a television company to make the series. He also got Will an **audition** for a leading role. The audition went well—Will got the part! His acting career had begun.

In *The Fresh Prince of Bel-Air*, Will's character often clashes with his rich cousin, Carlton (left).

Los Angeles was Will's new home and where *The Fresh Prince of Bel-Air* was filmed.

A family sitcom

The television series was called *The Fresh Prince of Bel-Air*. It was a **sitcom**, which meant that it was about funny events in a realistic setting. Will played the part of a confident teenager from Philadelphia. The humor comes from the fact that he goes to live with wealthy relatives in one of the richest parts of Los Angeles, called Bel-Air. His rich relatives try to make him behave better. Will's character has other ideas, and this often upsets them in a funny way.

At first, Will made a lot of mistakes as an actor. He spoke too quietly, forgot his lines, and looked into the camera. He had never acted before. However, Will was determined to learn. He studied the **professionals** he worked with and improved every day.

A TV hit

The Fresh Prince of Bel-Air won awards, and Will was voted favorite television actor in 1991. The series ran for six years. Will made sure Jeff had a part as his best friend.

Family life

In 1991 Will met a fashion design student called Sheree Zampino. They married a year later. In 1992, their son, Trey, was born.

Big screen

In 1992 Will got a small part in a movie called *Where the Day Takes You*. His second role was in a comedy movie called *Made in America*. The famous actress Whoopi Goldberg taught him that he must be more serious. Moviemakers have no time for actors who fool around between scenes. In *Made in America*, Will played a similar character to the one he played in *The Fresh Prince of Bel-Air*. He worried that he would always be given the same kind of role. His aim was to get a more serious part in a bigger movie.

Whoopi Goldberg and Will Smith acting in the movie *Made in America*.

Rapping live

Prepare your own **rap** performance. Your rap lyrics can be:

- lyrics you have written yourself (see page 15)
- Will Smith's lyrics (ask an adult to help you find some on the Internet)
- a nursery **rhyme** with a strong beat (for example, "Hey diddle diddle").

Steps to follow:

1. Get used to the beat. Experiment to find which words, or parts of words, the strong and weak beats fall on. Clapping as you say the words will help. Use a pencil to mark the strong beats.

2. Experiment with the sounds of the words. You could stretch out some words and break up or shorten others. You could also repeat parts of words. For example, "Hey diddle, diddle" could become "Heeey, did- did- diddle."

3. Rap artists often move to the beat, too. Relax and try to let your whole body get into the beat as you say the words.

4. Ask a friend to play the beat on a percussion instrument, or clap it out.

5. When you are happy with your rap, perform it in front of an audience.

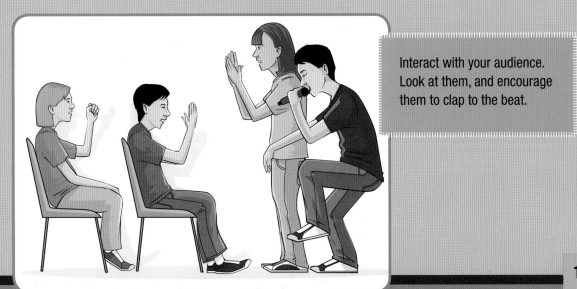

Interact with your audience. Look at them, and encourage them to clap to the beat.

In the Movies

Will Smith was delighted when he was given the leading role in a **drama** called *Six Degrees of Separation* in 1993. Dramas have a serious theme. Will played a character who tricks his way into the home of a wealthy family. It was a difficult role to perform. Will took acting lessons and worked hard. Will said of his work for *Six Degrees of Separation*, "My drive was the fact that … they didn't think that I could do it."

A smooth move into the movies

Will's hard work paid off. Movie critics praised his acting skills in *Six Degrees of Separation*. It was the beginning of Will's movie success. From then on, he was offered major roles in all kinds of movies.

Will plays a trickster in the drama *Six Degrees of Separation*.

Real-life drama

Six Degrees of Separation was based on a true story. Will later starred in another real-life movie that was a box-office hit. *Ali* (2001) was a **biography** of the boxing champion Muhammad Ali. Will had to copy the way Ali spoke, moved, and boxed! To look like the boxer, he had to build up his muscles in the gym.

Career first?

Will felt he had failed when he and Sheree divorced in 1995. Many people thought Will had put his career first and not spent enough time with his family. When he married again in 1997, he didn't make the same mistake. His new wife was actress Jada Pinkett. In 1998 they had a son, Jaden, and in 2000 they had a daughter, Willow.

To look like the boxer Muhammad Ali, Will had to gain 35 pounds (16 kilograms) and build up his muscles.

Action

In 1995 Will played an action hero for the first time, in a movie called *Bad Boys*. He played a wild cop and worked alongside **costar** Martin Lawrence, a comedian as well as an actor. The cops and robbers action involved a lot of running around and shooting. *Bad Boys* was a hit.

Sci-fi

Will's next challenge was a **sci-fi** action movie called *Independence Day* (1996). He played the role of a fighter pilot who had to stop aliens from invading Earth.

It was a box-office hit and soon brought in $800 million!

This poster is advertising *Independence Day*. After seeing the movie, people often stopped Will in the street to congratulate him.

Movie genres

Movies are described by their **genre** (the type of movie they are):
- Comedy: light-hearted plots; funny things are said and happen
- Drama: serious plots, often about realistic people and situations
- Sci-fi (or science fiction): usually set in outer space and/or the future
- Action: filled with exciting events, such as fights, car chases, and explosions.

Movies can be a mix of genres. For example, *Independence Day* is a sci-fi action movie.

Comedy

There is often a humorous element to Will's movies. *Men in Black* (1997) was a sci-fi comedy action movie. The movie was so successful that Will had the same role again in *Men in Black II*, in 2002.

A famous movie **producer**, Steven Spielberg, called Will to ask him to be in *Men in Black*. Will said yes, but he was a little worried about doing a second movie about aliens after *Independence Day*. This scene is from *Men in Black II*.

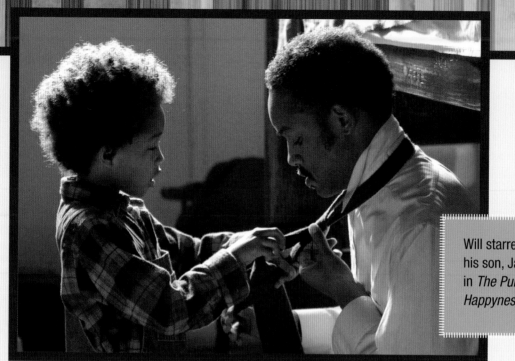

The amount of money Will earned as an actor rocketed. For his role in *Where the Day Takes You* (1992), he earned $50,000. For his role in *Men in Black II* (2002), he earned $20 million!

Awards and nominations

An **Oscar** is a major movie award. Will received two Oscar **nominations** for his parts in the movies *Ali* and *The Pursuit of Happyness*.

Overbrook Entertainment

Around 1997–99, Will started up his own company, Overbrook Entertainment. The company makes movies and television programs. It has produced hits starring Will, such as *The Pursuit of Happyness*. The company also manages artists and helps unknown music performers record music.

Oops!

Will has made a few mistakes. One was to turn down a lead role in *The Matrix*. Actor Keanu Reeves took the part instead. The movie was a massive hit.

Movie poster

Imagine that Will Smith is going to star in a new movie. It is your job to decide the movie's title and what it will be about. Finally, you have to design a poster to persuade people to go and see it!

Steps to follow:

1. What sort of movie would suit Will Smith? Pick a genre from the box on page 22.

2. What part would Will play? Describe the plot in a sentence. For example: "Will plays a cop who has to track down criminals who have stolen a deadly poison."

3. Think of an exciting title. A short title (such as *Wild Man Cop*) is more likely to grab people's attention than a longer title.

4. Sketch out your poster. Think about answers to these questions:

- How big should the movie title be?

- What kind of picture would be exciting? (A comedy movie would need a different kind of image than an action movie.)

- What colors best reflect the mood and plot? Try different materials (pens, paints, pastels).

5. Finish your poster. Ask your friends if they would go see this movie.

Don't clutter your poster with too much information. A simple, dramatic design is often the most eye-catching.

Multitalented

By working hard, Will achieved a successful movie career. But he remained a musician at the same time. He performed the theme songs for many of his movies, including *Men in Black*. Between 1997 and 2005 he brought out four solo **albums** and a *Greatest Hits* album.

African-American actor

As an African-American actor, Will has led the way for other African-Americans in Hollywood. *Bad Boys* (1995) was one of the first-ever action movies to star two leading African-American actors. In 2008 Will set the record for starring in the most consecutive (one after another) movies that each made $100 million at the box office. During his time as an actor, he has received about 30 awards and 50 **nominations**.

Will's fans live all around the world. Here, Will is signing autographs in New York.

Always busy

Will is always picking up new skills. He has been a **producer** as well an as actor, for movies such as *Hancock* and *Seven Pounds*. In 2008 he started to work on a role in his first epic movie, *The Last Pharaoh*.

His long list of wide-ranging skills includes fluently speaking Spanish and playing chess.

Family man

Although Will made a mistake with his first marriage by giving too much time to his career, he now puts his family first. Because he and his wife are both actors, they are both aware of the dangers of a Hollywood lifestyle. They protect their privacy and relationship. They live with their children in Los Angeles in a large home where Will has his own recording studio.

This picture shows Will with his daughter, Willow, and son Jaden.

Timeline

1968 Will Smith is born in Philadelphia, Pennsylvania, on September 25.

1989 **DJ** Jazzy Jeff and the Fresh Prince win their first major music award (a **Grammy**).

1990 Will takes a role in the TV **sitcom** *The Fresh Prince of Bel-Air*.

Will Smith became a multimillionaire while he was still a teenager.

1991 DJ Jazzy Jeff and the Fresh Prince win a second Grammy for "Summertime."

1992 Will marries Sheree Zampino; their son, Trey, is born.

1993 DJ Jazzy Jeff and the Fresh Prince release their last **album**, *Code Red*. Will appears in his first serious movie role in *Six Degrees of Separation*.

1995 Will stars as an action hero in *Bad Boys*. Sheree and Will divorce.

1996 Will stars in *Independence Day*.

1997	Will returns to music as a solo performer with *Big Willie Style*. He marries Jada Pinkett and stars in *Men in Black*.
1998	Will's son Jaden is born.
1999	Will stars in *Wild Wild West*, a comedy action movie.
2000	Will's daughter, Willow, is born.
2003	Will and Jada create and produce a sitcom called *All of Us*.
2004	Will produces and stars in the **sci-fi** movie *I, Robot*. He also stars in *Shark Tale*.
2005	Will produces and stars in the romantic comedy *Hitch*.
2007	Will receives an **Oscar nomination** for his role in *The Pursuit of Happyness*. He also stars in *I Am Legend*. His year's earnings are estimated to be $31 million.
2008	Will works as a **producer** on five movies.

Will Smith starred in the children's movie *Shark Tale*. He spoke the words of a little fish named Oscar.

Glossary

album record with several songs or pieces of music on it. Will has made four solo albums.

audition test that singers or actors do to show if they are good enough for a part in a movie or television program. Will passed his audition for *Six Degrees of Separation* and got the part.

biography story of a real person's life. *Ali* was a movie biography of a real boxer's life.

costar actor who plays alongside another star in a movie. Will costarred with actress Charlize Theron in *Hancock*.

disco music type of dance music. Clubs where disco music is played are sometimes called discos.

DJ (short for disc jockey) person who plays records. Rap DJs talk over the records they are playing. A rap DJ might also play the backing music while another artist (called an MC, or Master of Ceremonies) raps.

drama serious story

genre type of something. Movie genres range from Westerns to biographical dramas.

Grammy award for special achievements in music

hip-hop culture that includes fashion and a type of music. Hip-hop music uses rap.

inspiration something or someone who makes you want to achieve something similar. Will Smith might be an inspiration to actors who are just starting out in their career.

nomination honor that occurs when a person's name is suggested by others to win an award. Several people are usually nominated to win movie awards, such as the Oscars.

Oscar award given for achievements in moviemaking

producer person who helps make movies or albums. Producers are usually in charge of money in the making of a movie or album.

professional person who does a job for money

rap type of poetry that is spoken out loud. A musical beat is often played while the rap artist raps.

rhyme words with the same ending sound. *Hat* and *bat* rhyme.

rhythm regular or repeated beat in a poem, rap lyric, or piece of music

sci-fi (short for science-fiction) any story about the future or outer space. Sci-fi movies are often set in the future or involve spaceships and aliens.

single song that is sold on its own. A single is often brought out to help sell an album.

sitcom television series that is funny and set in a realistic setting, such as a home or office

tax money people have to pay to the government. The amount of tax you have to pay depends on how much money you earn.

Find Out More

Books

Hatch, Thomas. *A History of Hip-Hop: The Roots of Rap.* Bloomington, Minn.:
  Red Brick Learning, 2006.

Mack, Jim. *Hip-Hop* (*Culture in Action*). Chicago: Raintree, 2010.

Simone, Jacquelyn. *OutKast* (*Hip-Hop*). Broomall, Pa.: Mason Crest, 2008.

Uschan, Michael V. *Will Smith* (*People in the News*). Detroit: Lucent, 2009.

Websites

Will Smith Fan Club
www.fanpop.com/spots/will-smith
Fans of Will have created this website. It has lots of fun images and videos of Will.

The Official Will Smith Website
www.willsmith.com
This is Will Smith's own website. It contains information about all of Will's albums, movies, and other news.

Index